I0465383

From Home to Success:

Marketing Jobs for Everyone

CONTENTS:

Chapter 1: Introduction to Digital Marketing for Beginners

Chapter 2: Content Creation:The Power of Online Content

Chapter 3: Affiliate Marketing:A Beginner's Guide

Chapter 4: Social Media Marketing:From Zero to Influencer

Chapter 5: SEO and SEM:Making Your Work Visible

Chapter 6: Email Marketing: Building Relationships and Selling

Chapter 7: Marketing through Data Analytics: How to Use Data to Your Advantage

Chapter 8:Visual and Graphic Marketing:Creating a Visual Impact

Chapter 1: Introduction to Digital Marketing for Beginners

1.1:Overview of Digital Marketing

Digital marketing, or online marketing, encompasses all marketing efforts that use an online presence to engage current and prospective customers through digital channels such as search engines, social media, websites, email, and mobile apps. This guide is designed for those new to the digital marketing world, providing an overview that covers fundamental principles, common strategies, and emerging trends.

Foundations of Digital Marketing

Digital marketing leverages the ability to reach an audience in a targeted and personalized way, using data and technology to optimize campaigns and enhance engagement. Some of the foundational pillars include:

- *SEO (Search Engine Optimization):* The art of optimizing website content to improve visibility on search engines. This includes on-page techniques like keyword usage, and off-page like link building.
- *SEM (Search Engine Marketing):* Encompasses all marketing activities aimed at increasing visibility on search engines, often through paid campaigns (like Google AdWords).

- *Content Marketing:* Creating and distributing valuable, relevant content to attract and retain a clearly defined audience. This can include blogs, videos, infographics, and ebooks.

- *Social Media Marketing:* Utilizing social platforms to promote products or services, engage with customers, and build a community.

- *Email Marketing:* Sending commercial communications via email, which can include newsletters, special offers, or exclusive content.

Evolution and Trends

Digital marketing is constantly evolving, influenced by new technologies and shifts in consumer behavior. Currently, we are witnessing:

- *Influencer Marketing*: Collaborating with social media influencers to promote products or services, leveraging their credibility and follower base.

- *Data-Driven Marketing:* Using data analytics to segment audiences and personalize offers, enhancing campaign effectiveness.

- *AI and Machine Learning:* These tools are revolutionizing marketing by analyzing large data sets to predict purchasing behaviors, optimize campaigns in real-time, or create personalized content.

- *Real-Time Marketing*: Quickly responding to current events to create relevant, timely content that can boost engagement and virality.

- *E-commerce and Mobile Marketing*: With the rise of online sales and mobile device usage, digital marketing increasingly focuses on seamless and mobile-friendly shopping experiences.

Digital Marketing Strategies

For beginners, it's crucial to understand that an effective digital marketing strategy requires careful planning, which includes:

- *Defining Objectives:* Whether it's increasing brand visibility, generating leads, or selling directly, objectives should be SMART (Specific, Measurable, Achievable, Relevant, Time-bound).

- *Market and Audience Analysis:* Knowing your audience, their behaviors, preferences, and where they are online.

- *Creating an Editorial Calendar:* For content marketing, a schedule that outlines content creation and publication.

- *Tool and Platform Selection:* Choosing the right platforms and tools based on objectives and target audience.

- *Monitoring and Optimization:* Using analytics to measure performance and optimize campaigns based on collected data.

Challenges and Opportunities

Digital marketing faces challenges such as the constant need for updates, competition for online attention, and data privacy management. However, it also offers tremendous opportunities:

- *Global Reach:* The ability to reach a global audience with relatively low entry barriers.

- *Real-Time Feedback:* The capacity to receive immediate feedback from customers allows for quick strategy adjustments.

- Scalable Costs: Digital campaigns can be scaled up or down according to budget, with options ranging from zero-cost organic content marketing to paid advertising.

Conclusion
Digital marketing is a vast and dynamic field where the ability to adapt and innovate is key. For beginners, the key is to start with continuous learning, experiment with small projects to see what works, and above all, build an authentic online presence that resonates with your audience. With the right strategy, patience, and a deep understanding of digital dynamics, anyone can successfully navigate the digital marketing landscape.

1.2: Essential Tools and Platforms

Digital marketing requires a good grasp of the tools and platforms that facilitate campaign management, analysis, and execution. For beginners, here's a guide to essential tools and platforms that can make a difference:

1. Content Creation Tools
- *Canva:* An online graphic editor that allows you to create images, videos, presentations, and documents without advanced design skills. Ideal for infographics, social media posts, and promotional material.

- *Grammarly:* A grammatical correction tool that helps maintain a professional and consistent tone in written content, essential for blogs, emails, and websites.

2. SEO Tools
- *Google Search Console*: Provides data on how your website performs in Google search results, flagging any issues and offering optimization suggestions.

- *Ahrefs or SEMrush:* Advanced SEO analysis tools that offer data on keywords, backlinks, and competitor rankings. Useful for those looking to professionally optimize their site.

3. Social Media Platforms
- *Meta Business Suite:* Manages business pages on platforms like Instagram and

Facebook, offering posting tools, analytics, and community management features.

- *Twitter Ads*: For those wanting to boost visibility on Twitter, this platform allows for targeted advertising campaigns.

- *LinkedIn:* Not just a job search platform, but also a powerful B2B marketing tool with publishing and paid campaign features.

4. Email Marketing
- *Mailchimp*: Perhaps the most well-known email marketing platform, offering tools to create, send, and analyze email campaigns, with a free plan for small lists.

- *Sendinblue*: Similar to Mailchimp but with a more modern approach to digital communication, including SMS marketing and chat.

5. Analytics
- *Google Analytics*: Essential for tracking website traffic, understanding where it comes

from, and how users behave. Crucial for data-driven decisions.

- *Hotjar:* Adds depth with heatmaps, session recordings, and surveys, providing insights into how users interact with the site.

6. Website Creation and Management Tools

- *WordPress*: The most used platform for blogs and websites. With countless themes and plugins, it's perfect for those wanting an easily manageable and customizable website.

- *Wix or Squarespace:* For those preferring a "drag-and-drop" approach without coding, these platforms offer elegant solutions for creating custom websites.

7. Automation and Optimization Tools

- *Hootsuite or Buffer*: Useful for scheduling and posting content on social media automatically, allowing management of multiple accounts and monitoring analytics.

- *HubSpot:* More than a tool, it's a comprehensive platform offering CRM, marketing automation, sales tools, and analytics, all integrated.

8. Collaboration and Productivity Tools
- *Trello or Asana*:Useful for organizing marketing projects, assigning tasks, and tracking progress.

- *Slack*: For real-time team communication, with integration of various marketing and productivity tools.

9. Payment and Affiliate Tools
- *PayPal*: To facilitate online payments, whether for sales or affiliate transactions.

- *Rakuten Marketing or ShareASale*: Platforms that connect affiliates with merchants, allowing earnings through sales or actions generated by promotional links.

10. Education and Research Tools
- *Coursera or Udemy:* For those looking to enhance their skills, these platforms offer courses on every aspect of digital marketing, from SEO to data analytics.

- *Google Trends:* To analyze real-time search trends, helpful for creating relevant and trending content.

Conclusion

The world of digital marketing is vast and constantly evolving, and familiarity with the tools mentioned can provide a significant advantage. However, it's important to remember that the key to success doesn't just lie in using the tools, but in the ability to create an integrated strategy that uses these tools to effectively communicate with the target audience. For a beginner, starting with free tools or basic plans can be a great way to get comfortable, while investing in paid tools can offer advanced features and greater professionalism. Continuous learning and adapting to new technologies and trends are crucial to staying competitive in the dynamic world of digital marketing.

1.3: How to Start with a Limited Budget

Digital marketing has become an essential component for any business looking to expand its online presence and reach a broader audience. However, for those with a limited budget, the challenge is finding effective strategies without having to spend considerable sums. Here's a beginner's guide to starting your digital marketing journey with limited resources.

1. Understand the Basics

First and foremost, it's crucial to understand that digital marketing isn't solely based on large advertising investments. Many of its most effective strategies are grounded in creativity, strategy, and smart use of free or low-cost platforms. The basics include:

- *SEO (Search Engine Optimization):*
Optimizing your website for search engines. This doesn't require large expenses but time and knowledge. Using free tools like Google Analytics and Google Search Console can help monitor and improve your site's ranking.

- _Content Marketing_: Creating valuable content that attracts and engages your audience. This can be done through blogs, videos, infographics, which can be distributed for free on social media.

- _Social Media Marketing:_ Utilizing social platforms to interact with your audience. While paid advertising on these platforms can be effective, starting with organic posts can already yield good results.

2. Low-Cost Strategies
SEO
- _Keyword Research_: Use tools like Google Keyword Planner, which is free, to understand which keywords to use.
- _Quality Content_: Write articles and pages that answer your audience's questions. Content quality is crucial for improving SEO.

Content Marketing
- _Blogging_: Create a blog associated with your website. Blogs can bring organic traffic and improve SEO.
- _Email Marketing:_ While it might seem old-fashioned, email marketing is still very

effective. You can start with free tools like Mailchimp for your initial campaigns.

Social Media
- *Organic Posts:* Before investing in ads, focus on organic posts. The key is interaction: respond to comments, create polls, and engage the community.
- *Collaborations:* Collaborate with influencers or other companies with similar budgets for co-marketing campaigns.

3. Use Free Tools
- *Google Ads Grant:* If you have a nonprofit organization, Google offers a $10,000 monthly grant for free advertising. Even though it's not exactly "free" for everyone, it shows there are ways to gain visibility without huge expenses.
- *Canva:* For creating high-quality graphics without high costs.
- *Hootsuite or Buffer*: To schedule social media posts for free up to a certain number of accounts.

4. Invest in Education
Even with a limited budget, investing in your education is crucial. There are many online

resources available for free or at low cost:

- *MOOCs (Massive Open Online Courses):* Platforms like Coursera, Udemy (often with deals), and Khan Academy offer digital marketing courses.
- *YouTube and Blogs*: Many experts share advice for free. Channels like those of Neil Patel or HubSpot Academy provide valuable content.

5. Analysis and Adaptation
- *Analytics:* Use Google Analytics to understand where your traffic comes from, which content works, and which doesn't. This allows you to adapt your strategy without additional costs.
- *A/B Testing*: Test different versions of a post, landing page, or email to see what works best.

6. Networking
- *Online Event Participation*: Many digital events are free or low-cost. These offer networking opportunities, learning new strategies, and getting known.

- *Forums and Groups*: Engage in discussions on Reddit, LinkedIn, or marketing-focused groups on platforms like X.

7. Retargeting Strategies
- *Economical Retargeting:* Even though retargeting might require a small investment, tools like Google Ads or social media allow targeting people who have already interacted with you, increasing conversion chances.

8. Affiliation and Partnerships
- *Affiliate Marketing*: You can earn without substantial expenses by promoting other companies' products. This not only can generate income but also increase your brand's visibility.

9. Focus on Community Building
- *Community Creation*: Utilize platforms like Discord to build a community around your brand. This can generate engagement and valuable feedback without extra costs.

Conclusion

Digital marketing with a limited budget requires creativity, dedication, and a well-thought-out strategy. Start with the basics of SEO and content marketing, maximize free resources, invest in yourself through education, and don't underestimate the importance of networking and data analysis. Over time, these practices will allow you to grow your online presence without significant expenses, demonstrating that success in digital marketing isn't just a matter of money, but how you use it.

Chapter 2: Content Creation:The Power of Online Content

2.1: Blog and Article Creation

In the digital jungle of the 21st century, content is king. Creating quality blogs and articles is not just an art, but a science that can turn casual readers into a devoted audience, and more importantly, loyal customers. This chapter explores the importance of content creation, focusing particularly on blog and article creation, an art that requires a blend of creativity, strategy, and a deep understanding of one's target market.

Why Create Blogs and Articles?

1. *Visibility and SEO*: Search engines like Google reward websites with high-quality, frequently updated content. A well-maintained blog can improve SEO (Search Engine Optimization), making the site more visible and accessible to users searching for specific terms.

2. _Engagement_: Blogs offer a direct means of interacting with the audience. Comments, social shares, and immediate feedback help build a community around the brand.

3. _Positioning as an Expert:_ Publishing in-depth, informative articles positions the author as an expert in their field. This not only increases reader trust but can also open doors to collaborations and business opportunities.

4. _Lead Generation_: Through the use of call-to-actions, blogs can guide readers to subscribe to newsletters, download free resources, or purchase products, turning visitors into qualified leads.

Effective Content Creation Strategies

1. Know Your Audience

Before writing a single word, it's crucial to understand who your readers will be.
   - _Reader Persona:_ Create a persona for your ideal reader. What are their interests,

problems, and how do they express themselves online?

- _Keyword Research:_ Use tools like Google Keyword Planner to discover what users are searching for and the questions they are asking.

2. Content Planning

A successful blog is never random.

- _Editorial Calendar_: Plan topics, publication dates, and collaborations in advance. This helps maintain thematic coherence and publication frequency.

- _Recurring Themes_: Identify topics that recur in your industry and create series of articles that can be published regularly.

3. Content Quality

- _Originality:_ Write content that offers a new perspective or solution to the reader's problems. Copying or paraphrasing others is not only ethically wrong but also harmful to SEO.

- _Length and Depth_: Sometimes, brevity is better, but longer, detailed articles can come across as more authoritative and are often favored in search results.

4. Style and Tone

- *Brand Voice:* Develop a tone that reflects the brand. It could be professional, friendly, witty, but it must be consistent.
- *Storytelling:* Use stories, real-life examples, and anecdotes to make posts more engaging. Human narrative is a powerful tool for connection.

5. Search Engine Optimization (SEO)

- *Titles and Meta-description:* Write titles that grab attention and accurately describe the article's content.
- *Keyword Use:* Integrate keywords strategically into the text without overdoing it. Natural language is key.
- *Content Structure*: Use subheadings (H2, H3), bullet lists, and bold text to facilitate reading and improve SEO.

6. Interactivity and Multimedia

- *Visuals:* Images, infographics, videos not only make content more appealing but also more shareable.
- *Interactivity:* Incorporating quizzes, polls, or FAQ sections can increase site dwell time, enhancing SEO.

Challenges and Solutions

Content creation isn't without challenges

- *Maintaining Innovation:* The risk of repetition. **Solution**: Follow trends, attend webinars, collaborate with other creators for fresh ideas.
- *Time Management:* Content creation is time-consuming. **Solution**: Plan well in advance, use automation tools, and consider outsourcing some tasks.
- *Negative Feedback:* Not all posts will be well-received. **Solution**: Respond constructively, view feedback as an opportunity for improvement.

Conclusion

Blog and article creation is both an art and a science that, when done well, can transform how a brand communicates and relates to its audience. It's a continuous journey of learning, adapting, and innovating, where every written word is a step towards success. Remember, content not only informs but builds relationships, and in an increasingly digital world, these relationships can make the difference between fleeting success and lasting achievement.

Chapter 2.2: Guide to Video and Podcast Production

In the vast and dynamic landscape of digital marketing, video and podcast production has taken on a central role. These mediums not only capture attention in ways text cannot but also offer a more personal and engaging experience. This chapter explores how to create effective videos and podcasts for marketing, from concept to publication.

The Importance of Videos and Podcasts

- Emotional Connectivity: Videos and podcasts allow for an emotional connection with the audience, offering a human dimension to the brand that is hard to achieve through writing alone.
- _Versatility_: Videos can be used on platforms like YouTube, Instagram, TikTok, while podcasts are ideal for commuters or those who prefer multitasking.
- _SEO and Sharing_: Both formats are easily shareable, and if optimized, can improve search engine rankings.

Video Production

1. _Planning and Pre-production_

   - _Define the Objective:_ Whether it's for entertainment, information, or branding, every video should have a clear goal.
   - _Script and Storyboard_: Even for the shortest videos, having a script and storyboard helps maintain focus and visual coherence.
   - _Trend Research_: Analyze what's currently working on platforms like YouTube or TikTok.

Trends change quickly, so staying updated is essential.

2. *Shooting and Post-production*

- *Equipment:* You don't need the best equipment, but good audio and video quality are crucial. A decent microphone and a quality camera or smartphone will do.
- *Editing:* Use software like Adobe Premiere, Final Cut, or even less costly options like iMovie or Shotcut. Editing can turn mediocre footage into high-quality content.
- *Visual Elements:* Add text, graphics, transitions. These elements not only make the video look more professional but also more engaging.

3. *Optimization and Distribution*

- *Video SEO*: Titles, tags, descriptions, and thumbnails are crucial for SEO. Use relevant keywords.
- *Promotion*: It's not enough just to upload a video; it needs to be promoted through social media, email marketing, and collaborations.

Podcast Production

1. *Preparation*

- *Format*: Decide if it will be a talk show, a series of interviews, a monologue, or a combination.
- *Topics:* Choose subjects that interest your target market, perhaps answering common questions in your industry.

2. *Recording*

- *Audio Setup:* Investing in a good microphone is essential. Even a treated acoustic environment can make a difference.
- *Recording Software*: Audacity, GarageBand, or more professionally, Reaper, are great for starting out.
- *Script or Key Points:* Even though the podcast can be spontaneous, having a plan helps keep the conversation on track.

3. *Post-production*
- *Editing:* Cut long pauses, mistakes, and add background music or sound effects.

- *Mastering:* Ensure the volume is consistent and without peaks. Tools like Auphonic can automate this process.

4. *Publication*

- *Platforms:* Distribute the podcast on platforms like Spotify, Apple Podcasts, Google Podcasts.
- *Artwork and Descriptions:* An attractive cover and clear description are essential to attract listeners.

Challenges and Strategies

- *Quality vs. Quantity*: Is it better to publish high-quality content less frequently or more content of lower quality? The answer depends on the target audience, but quality tends to prevail in the long run.
- *Feedback and Adaptation:* Listen to your audience. Comments, reviews, and view analytics can guide improvements.
- *Collaborations*: Collaborating with other creators can expand your audience and offer new perspectives and content.

Conclusion

Producing videos and podcasts requires creativity, planning, and a bit of technical know-how. However, investing in these media can offer significant returns in terms of visibility, engagement, and audience loyalty. In the race toward online success, videos and podcasts are not only marketing tools; they are means to build authentic connections, tell stories, and create a lasting digital footprint. Remember, success doesn't come overnight but from a consistent commitment to learning, adapting, and improving your production.

Chapter 2.3: Strategies for Generating and Maintaining Engagement

In the vast digital ocean, content is the ship that sails through the waves of user attention. Creating content that not only catches the eye but also the interest and engagement of the audience is crucial for marketing success. Here's an overview of the most effective strategies for generating and maintaining online engagement.

1. Know Your Audience
Before creating any content, it's essential to understand who your audience is. Analyze your users:

  - _Demographics_: Age, gender, occupation, income.
  - _Behaviors:_ How they interact with content, which platforms they prefer, when they are most active.
  - _Interests:_ Topics they are passionate about, problems they are trying to solve.

Knowing your audience allows you to create relevant and customized content, thus boosting engagement.

2. Interesting and Authentic Stories
Stories capture attention and create an emotional bond. Be authentic:

  - _Brand Narrative_: Tell your brand's story, its values, struggles, and successes.

- *Testimonials and Case Studies:* Use customer or user success stories.
- *Human Content:* Show the human face behind the brand with vlogs, behind-the-scenes, or interviews.

Authentic stories not only increase engagement but also build trust and loyalty among your audience.

3. Diverse Content Formats

Variety is the spice of life, especially online. Use various formats:

- *Video:* Tutorials, vlogs, live streams.
- *Text:* Articles, blogs, guides.
- *Images:* Infographics, photographs, memes.
- *Audio:* Podcasts, short audio clips.

Each format has its audience and can reach people at different times of the day. Offering a variety of content helps maintain interest.

4. Interactivity

Engaging your audience with interactive content is a great way to maintain engagement:

- *Quizzes and Polls*: Ask for opinions or test your audience's knowledge.
- *Polls*: Collaborative decisions on future content or products.
- *Comments and Discussions:* Promote discussion with open-ended questions or controversial topics.

Interactivity not only boosts engagement but also provides valuable feedback.

5. Use of Hashtags and Trends

Leverage the power of trends and hashtags:

- *Trends:* Participate in viral challenges, fashion trends, or current events.
- *Hashtags:* Create specific hashtags for campaigns or use popular ones to increase visibility.
This not only increases engagement but can also reach a broader audience.

6. Consistency and Frequency

Consistency and frequency are crucial. Establish a publication schedule:

- *Planning:* Plan posts in advance to maintain a constant presence.
- *Frequency*: Find a frequency that works for your audience (daily, weekly).

A regular schedule keeps the audience engaged and looking forward to your next content.

7. SEO and Analytics

Use SEO (Search Engine Optimization) techniques to ensure your content is easily found:

- *Keyword Research*: Find relevant keywords and use them.
- *On-Page SEO*: Optimize titles, descriptions, tags.
- *Analytics:* Use tools like Google Analytics to understand which content performs best.

Analytics allows you to continuously adapt your strategy to maximize engagement.

8. Collaborations and Partnerships

Collaborating with others creates synergy that can bring new followers and more engagement:

  - *Influencers*: Collaborations with influencers who share your target audience.
  - *Cross-Promotion*: Content swaps or mentions with other brands.

These collaborations can lead to a wider and more diverse audience.

9. Feedback and Adaptation

Listen to your audience:

  - *Respond to Comments*: Interact with comments, answer questions.
  - *Feedback*: Ask for opinions on your content and be ready to adapt.

Adapting based on feedback is key to maintaining long-term engagement.

10. Innovation and Experimentation

Don't be afraid to experiment:

- *New Formats*: Try new types of content or platforms.
- *Technology*: Use new technologies like AR/VR to create immersive experiences.

Innovation keeps your content fresh and interesting.

Conclusion

Generating and maintaining online engagement requires a blend of strategy, creativity, and adaptability. Knowing your audience, telling authentic stories, diversifying formats, being interactive, and staying consistent are foundational pillars. Using SEO, collaborating, gathering feedback, and not being afraid to experiment complete the picture. Remember, engagement isn't just about numbers; it's about human connections built through content.

Chapter 3: Affiliate Marketing:

A Beginner's Guide

3.1:How Affiliate Marketing Works

Affiliate marketing is one of the most popular and accessible forms of online marketing, especially for those new to the world of online earning. This chapter will guide you through the basic mechanisms of this strategy, explaining how it works, its advantages, and how you can start generating income through it.

What is Affiliate Marketing?

Affiliate marketing, also known as performance marketing, is a business model where an affiliate promotes the products or services of another individual or company (termed the "advertiser" or "brand") and earns a commission for every sale, click, lead, or specific action generated through their unique affiliate link. This system is based on an agreement between the affiliate and the advertiser, where the affiliate commits to driving traffic to the advertiser's site, and the advertiser commits to paying for the actions generated.

How It Works

1. *Joining an Affiliate Program:* To start, you need to sign up for an affiliate program. There are platforms like Amazon Associates, Commission Junction, or ShareASale, which offer a wide range of products and services to promote. Once registered, you receive a unique link that identifies you as an affiliate.

2. *Promotion:* Using your affiliate link, you can promote products or services in various ways: through a blog, social media, email marketing, YouTube videos, or any other channel that reaches your audience. The key is to create engaging and relevant content that encourages your audience to click on your links.

3. *Tracking and Payment:* When someone clicks on your link and performs the desired action (like making a purchase, signing up for

a service, or downloading something), this action is tracked. Tracking systems ensure that each sale or action is correctly attributed to the right affiliate. At the end of a set period (usually monthly or quarterly), the affiliate receives their payment.

Types of Payment Models

- *Pay Per Sale (PPS)*: You earn a commission only if the click on your link results in a sale.
- *Pay Per Lead (PPL)*: You get paid for each lead generated, such as a signup or newsletter subscription.
- *Pay Per Click (PPC)*: You are paid for each click on your link, regardless of any subsequent action.
- *Hybrid Models*: Some programs combine two or more of these models to offer a more flexible payment structure.

Advantages of Affiliate Marketing

- *Low Barrier to Entry:* You don't need your own product or manage inventory. You can start with minimal technical tools, often just a website or blog.

- *Scalability:* You can start small and scale your activities as you gain more experience and resources.
- *Diversification:* You're not limited to a single product or brand. You can promote a variety of products or services, thus reducing risks associated with a single business.
- *Passive Income:* Once content is online and starts generating traffic and sales, the initial work can turn into passive income.

Tips for Success in Affiliate Marketing

- *Niche Selection*: Start by focusing on a specific niche. This allows you to become an expert in your field, increasing your audience's trust.
- *Create Valuable Content*: Content quality is crucial. Write in-depth reviews, guides, or tutorials that solve your readers' problems. Valuable content attracts organic traffic and increases conversion rates.
- *SEO and SEM:* Optimize your content for search engines (SEO) and consider using paid advertising (SEM) to boost traffic.
- *Analysis and Optimization*: Use tools like Google Analytics to monitor which links and content generate more clicks and sales.

Continuously optimize your strategy based on the gathered data.
- _Relationships with Advertisers_: Build strong relationships with advertisers. Sometimes, affiliate programs offer special deals or better commissions for those who prove to deliver good results.

Conclusion

Affiliate marketing offers an exceptional opportunity for anyone looking to enter the digital marketing world with a relatively low initial investment. The key to success lies in choosing the right niche, content quality, continuous analysis, and strategy optimization. With dedication and the right strategy, affiliate marketing can become a significant income source, turning personal interest or passion into a lucrative career. Remember, like any business form, success isn't guaranteed overnight, but with time and effort, the growth potential is nearly limitless.

Chapter 3.2: Product and Platform Selection

One of the most critical aspects of succeeding in affiliate marketing is choosing the right products and platforms through which to promote them. The selection of items or services you'll promote directly affects your conversion rate, while the platforms determine how easily and effectively you can manage your affiliate business. Here's a detailed guide on how to proceed.

Product Selection

1. *Know Your Audience:* First and foremost, you need a clear understanding of your audience. What are their needs, desires, and problems? Promoting products that address these issues is crucial. If your blog is about travel, promoting travel accessories or booking services could be very effective.

2. *Personalization and Relevance*: Products must be relevant to the content you publish. Content consistency with promoted products

increases trust and purchase intent. For example, if you write tech product reviews, promotions for smartphone accessories or photo editing software might be pertinent.

3. *Quality and Reputation:* Promoting high-quality products not only increases your audience's trust in you but can also lead to positive reviews that further boost sales. Look for brands with a good reputation and products with positive reviews.

4. *Price and Perceived Value:* Consider the price of the products. Items with a good quality-to-price ratio or that offer high perceived value tend to convert better, especially if your audience is price-sensitive.

5. *Commissions and Payout Structure:* Analyze the commissions offered. Some products might come with higher commissions or more advantageous payment structures. However, don't choose a product solely for the commission; relevance and quality should be priorities.

Choosing Affiliate Platforms

Choosing the right affiliate platform is equally vital. Here are some key selection criteria:

1. *Reputation and Reliability:* Platforms like Amazon Associates, ShareASale, or ClickBank are well-established and offer a wide range of products. Their reliability is a plus, especially for beginners, as they ensure timely payments and adequate support.

2. *Product Variety*: Some platforms specialize in certain niches. For instance, if you're in the health and wellness sector, platforms offering such products could be more beneficial.

3. *Support and Tools*: Consider the level of support provided and tools available. Good platforms offer advanced tracking tools, quick customer support, and resources for affiliates like banners, links, and promotional materials.

4. *Payout Conditions*: Each platform has its payment policies, including minimum payout

thresholds, payment frequency, and transfer methods. Choose those that best meet your financial needs.

5. *Compliance and Transparency:* Ensure the platform is transparent about its policies, especially regarding user data and privacy. Compliance with advertising and affiliate regulations is crucial to avoid legal issues.

Strategies for Product Selection

- *Testing and Trials*: Don't hesitate to try products yourself. Personal reviews or genuine testimonials increase audience trust.
- *Audience Feedback:* Use your channels to ask your audience directly what they're looking for or which products they'd like to see reviewed.
- *Market Analysis:* Keep an eye on market trends. New or increasingly popular products can offer an initial competitive edge.

Conclusion

Selecting products and affiliate platforms is an art that requires research, analysis, and, most importantly, an intimate knowledge of your audience. Start with a few quality products that you know meet a real demand from your audience. Expand your offering as you gain more experience and feedback. Remember, success in affiliate marketing doesn't just depend on your promotional skills but also on the savvy in choosing what to promote and where to do it. With the right strategy, affiliate marketing can turn into an enjoyable and profitable income source.

Chapter 3.3: Ethical and Profitable Promotion Techniques

Affiliate marketing is one of the most accessible and lucrative forms of digital marketing for anyone wanting to start an online business. However, to succeed without compromising your ethics or those of your users, it's essential to adopt promotion techniques that are both ethical and profitable. In this chapter, we'll explore how to do just that.

1. Choose Products or Services You Know and Believe In

The foundation of ethical affiliate marketing is promoting products or services that you would use yourself or believe in. This not only makes you more credible in the eyes of your audience but allows you to speak with more passion and authenticity. If you promote something you haven't tested or don't like, your enthusiasm and authenticity will be compromised, and your audience will notice.

2. Always Disclose Your Affiliate Relationship

Transparency is key. The FTC (Federal Trade Commission) in the U.S., and similar regulations worldwide, require that you clearly disclose your affiliate relationship when promoting a product. This might seem like a hurdle, but it actually increases your audience's trust. The phrase "This post contains affiliate links" or the use of hashtags like #affiliatelink can suffice.

3. Create Valuable Content

Content should always be at the heart of your strategy. Offer in-depth reviews, useful guides, tutorials, or product comparisons. When content is valuable, users are more likely to trust you and follow your recommendations, increasing the likelihood of conversion. Remember, user value comes first.

4. Use Multiple Promotion Channels

Don't limit yourself to one channel. You can use blogs, YouTube videos, podcasts, social media, and even email marketing. Diversifying channels not only increases visibility but allows you to reach different audience segments. For example, a YouTube video can visually explain a product, while an Instagram post can capture attention with attractive images.

5. SEO and Content Marketing

Search engine optimization (SEO) is crucial for getting your content found. Use relevant keywords, create internal and external links, and ensure your articles are well-structured and easy to read. Content marketing, like regularly posting blog articles, not only improves your SEO but also builds a content library that can generate traffic over time.

6. Ethical Email Marketing

Email marketing can be powerful, but it must be done ethically. Don't buy email lists, but build them organically through opt-ins. Send emails only with relevant and useful content, and always with an easy opt-out option. Emails should be informative, not just promotional, to keep subscribers engaged.

7. Collaborations and Influencer Marketing

Collaborating with other content creators or influencers can expand your audience. However, it's important these collaborations are transparent and that influencers share your values and ethics. The audience is increasingly aware of who promotes what and with what authenticity.

8. Continuous Analysis and Adaptation

Ethics in affiliate marketing isn't just about how you promote but also how you optimize your strategies. Continuously analyze the performance of your affiliate links, user behavior, and adapt your approaches. If a product isn't converting, it might not be suitable for your audience, or perhaps your promotional method isn't effective.

9. Educate Your Audience on Affiliate Marketing

Often, consumers don't understand how affiliate marketing works. Spend time explaining how you earn through affiliate links and why this doesn't affect the quality of the product or service. An informed audience is more likely to support your efforts.

10. Build a Community

Lastly, ethics in affiliate marketing also manifest in building an authentic community. Engage with your followers, respond to comments, ask for opinions and feedback. A community isn't just an audience; it's a group of people who support you and whom you commit to offering continuous value.

Conclusion

Affiliate marketing can be extremely profitable, but ethics should not be sacrificed for profit. Promoting products you believe in, maintaining transparency, creating valuable content, and building genuine relationships with your audience are the keys to lasting success. Remember, the real value in affiliate marketing doesn't just come from commissions, but from the trust and respect you build with your audience.

Chapter 4: Social Media Marketing: From Zero to Influencer

4.1:Utilizing Social Platforms for Marketing

Social media marketing has become a fundamental pillar for any digital marketing strategy. Social platforms allow companies and individuals to reach a vast audience with targeted, interactive, and personalized content. This chapter will explore how to best leverage social platforms to transform from zero to influencer.

1. Understanding Social Platforms

Before starting, it's essential to understand that each social platform has its own culture, demographics, and set of features. Here's an overview:

- _Instagram_: Ideal for visual content. Use stories, IGTV, Reels, and feed posts to connect with your audience. Great for fashion, travel, and lifestyle.

- *X (Twitter)*: Perfect for news, real-time updates, and conversations. X is where the community discusses, shares opinions, and follows trends.

- *LinkedIn:* The professional platform to connect with colleagues, B2B clients, and build industry reputation.

- *YouTube*: The domain of video content. Great for tutorials, reviews, and educational content. Has immense potential for monetization.

- *TikTok*: The emerging platform for short, creative content. Perfect for trends, entertainment, and reaching a young audience.

- *Pinterest and Reddit:* More niche but powerful for inspiration, education, and specific communities.

2. Creating a Business Profile

The first step is creating a professional or business profile. Ensure that:

- The bio is clear and engaging: With a link to your website or YouTube channel.
- The profile and cover images are high quality: Reflecting your brand or professional personality.
- Contact information is visible: To facilitate collaboration and sales.

3. Valuable Content

The heart of social media marketing is content. It should be:

- Relevant: To your target audience.
- Educational or Entertaining: Adds value or makes people smile.
- Consistent: Maintain a regular schedule to keep engagement up.

Use stories, short videos, live sessions, and posts to vary content types and keep interest alive.

4. Engagement and Interaction

Engagement is everything. Respond to comments, participate in discussions, and create content that invites interaction (polls, quizzes, Q&A).
- *Create Community*: Groups on X or Instagram can be excellent for building a more engaged follower base.

5. Collaborations and Influencer Marketing

Collaborating with other creators or influencers can amplify your reach.

- *Niche Influencers:* Choose influencers with an audience similar to your target market.
- *Cross-Platform Collaborations:* Use the strength of multiple platforms to maximize exposure.

6. Hashtag and Social SEO Strategies

Hashtags and keywords help discover your content to new users.

- *Hashtag Research:* Use tools like Hashtagify to find popular and relevant hashtags.
- *Social SEO*: Optimize video descriptions on YouTube or posts on X to improve visibility.

7. Analysis and Optimization
Use the analytics tools provided by platforms to understand what works and what doesn't.

- *Insights and Analytics*: Look at which content gets the most engagement and adjust your strategy accordingly.
- *A/B Testing:* Test different types of content or posts to see which performs best.

8. Using Ads to Amplify

Social media ad campaigns can significantly boost growth, even with initially limited budgets.

- *Targeted Ads*: Use demographic data, interests, and behavior to target ads to the right people.
- *Retargeting:* Reach people who have already interacted with your content to increase conversions.

9. Maintaining Credibility and Trust

Your audience's trust is crucial. Maintain transparent communication, respect privacy, and respond promptly to any criticism or negative feedback.

10. Continuous Growth

The social media world changes quickly. Continue educating yourself, follow trends, and adapt your strategy. The key is to stay relevant and innovative.

Conclusion

Social media marketing isn't just about posting content. It's about building a presence, a community, and an influence. With the right strategy, anyone can transform from a beginner to an influencer, leveraging the enormous opportunities social platforms offer. Remember, the key is authenticity, consistency, and adaptability.

Chapter 4.2: Building a Following Community

Success in social media marketing isn't just about numbers; it's about building a loyal and engaged community. In this chapter, we'll explore strategies to create and maintain a community that not only follows your content but feels part of something larger.

1. Define Your Niche

Firstly, it's essential to know who you are and who your audience is. Identifying a specific niche allows you to create relevant content and attract followers who are genuinely interested in what you offer. The niche could be based on an interest, an industry, a lifestyle, or a specific problem you intend to solve.

- *Example*: If you're passionate about vegan cooking, your niche could be "Easy and Healthy Vegan Recipes". This helps you focus your content on themes that attract vegans or people interested in a vegan diet.

2. Create Quality Content

Content quality is the heartbeat of any community. Your posts need to be not only informative but also engaging, visually appealing, and useful.

- *Videos*: Tutorials, vlogs, behind-the-scenes.
- *Images*: Professional photos, infographics, carousels.
- *Text:* Articles, tips, personal stories.

3. Interact Authentically

Posting isn't enough; it's crucial to interact with your followers. Responding to comments, participating in discussions, and showing gratitude for support creates a personal connection.

- *Example:* If someone comments on one of your posts about a recipe, respond with a thank you and perhaps a suggestion on how to personalize it. This not only shows that you care about their opinion but that you're open to dialogue.

4. Use Stories and Reels

Stories and Reels on Instagram, for example, are powerful tools for increasing engagement. They are more ephemeral but often more engaging because they are more personal and immediate.

- *Stories*: Share moments from your day, sneak peeks of projects, or answer followers' questions.
- *Reels:* Create short and fun content that can easily go viral, increasing your profile's visibility.

5. Collaborations and Partnerships

Collaborating with other influencers or brands in your niche can organically expand your following. Collaborations should be authentic and beneficial for both parties.

- _Example_: A vegan chef might collaborate with an organic ingredient brand for a series of exclusive recipes.

6. Organize Events or Webinars

Virtual events or webinars are great for engaging your community more deeply. These can be Q&A sessions, workshops, or discussions on topics relevant to your niche.

- _Live Events_: Live cooking streams where followers can participate in real-time with questions and suggestions.

7. Leverage Hashtags and Trends

Hashtags are crucial for making your content

discoverable. Use both niche-specific and trending hashtags to increase visibility.

- *Example*: #VeganRecipe, #HealthyLiving, #Foodie, in addition to seasonal or event-related hashtags like #Veganuary.

8. Create an Offline Community

Don't underestimate the power of physical meetups or local events. If possible, organize meetups, dinners, or markets where your followers can see you in person and interact with each other.

- *Example*: A monthly vegan cooking meetup where participants can cook together and share their creations.

9. Feedback and Continuous Improvement

Collecting feedback from your followers is crucial for continuous improvement. Use polls, questions in posts, or stories to understand what works and what doesn't.

- *Example*: Questions like "What's your favorite type of recipe?" can guide your future content creation.

10. Maintain Consistency

Consistency in tone, quality, and frequency of your posts is key. Your followers expect a certain type of content and should be able to rely on your presence.

- *Planning:* Use scheduling tools to maintain a steady flow of content without stress.

Conclusion

Building a following community on social media requires time, effort, and a well-thought-out strategy. It's not just about accumulating numbers but creating an environment where your niche feels at home, engaged, and valued. Remember that every interaction is an opportunity to strengthen the bond with your audience. With dedication and authenticity, you'll not only grow as an influencer but also make a positive and lasting impact in your community.

Chapter 4.3: Analysis and Optimization of Social Media Campaigns

Analysis and optimization of social media campaigns are foundational pillars for anyone looking not only to build but also to maintain an influential online presence. This process is continuous, dynamic, and requires a deep understanding of metrics, tools, and market trends. Here's a detailed guide on how to analyze and optimize your campaigns.

1. Define Clear Objectives

First and foremost, it's essential to have clear objectives. Whether it's to increase follower count, improve engagement, drive clicks to your website, or generate sales, each goal requires a specific approach.

- *Example*: If the goal is to increase sales, you should focus campaigns on content that drives qualified traffic to the product page.

2. Preliminary Analysis

Before starting a new campaign or optimizing an existing one, conducting a preliminary analysis is crucial. This includes:

- *Audience Analysis*: Who are your followers? What interests them? What are their content and platform preferences?
- *Benchmarking:* Compare your performance with competitors. What strategies work for them?

3. Use of Analytics Tools

Analytics tools like Sprout Social, Google Analytics, or social media AI platforms provide valuable data. These tools help to:

- *Monitor Performance:* Evaluate which posts receive the most engagement, which hashtags are effective, and how engagement varies over time.

- *Sentiment Analysis:* Use AI to understand the audience's opinion on your content, which can influence future strategy.

4. Content Optimization

Content optimization is an art that refines over time. Here are some key points:

- *Content Types*: Diversify between text, images, videos, live sessions, stories. Each content type has its moment and audience.
- *Timing and Frequency:* Analyze when your audience is most active and adjust content posting to these time windows.
- *Interactivity*: Encourage interaction with questions, polls, and content that asks for feedback.

5. Feedback and Iteration

Analysis isn't an event but a process.
Collecting feedback through comments, direct messages, or polls is vital. This allows you to:

- *Adapt Strategy*: If a type of content isn't working, change your approach. If a topic is hot, delve deeper into it.
- *Continuous Growth:* Learning from past campaigns is essential to improve future ones.

6. A/B Testing

A/B testing is a powerful tool for optimization. Test different versions of posts, different posting times, or variations in copy and images to see what works best.

- *Example*: Publish two versions of a post with slight differences and analyze which receives more engagement.

7. Scalability

Once you've found strategies that work, think about how to scale them. This could mean increasing the ad budget, collaborating with larger influencers, or expanding the content creator team.

8. Use of Technologies

AI and automation are revolutionizing social media marketing. Using tools like Ultimamente, which can generate content based on your archives, can enhance the efficiency and relevance of your posts.

Conclusion

The analysis and optimization of social media campaigns require a methodical and dynamic approach. It's not just about launching content and hoping for success but about continuous evolution based on data, feedback, and innovation. By using the right tools, maintaining an active dialogue with your audience, and adapting to trends, you can transform your social media presence from just an account to a true influencer in your industry. Remember, success in social media is a marathon, not a sprint; every step of optimization brings you closer to your goal

Chapter 5: SEO and SEM:Making Your Work Visible

5.1: Introduction to SEO

Search Engine Optimization (SEO) is a critical discipline in digital marketing aimed at enhancing a website's visibility on search engines like Google. The goal of SEO is to rank a website in the top positions of search results for relevant keywords, thereby increasing organic traffic, brand visibility, and ultimately, conversions.

Why is SEO Important?

- *Organic Traffic:* Traffic from search engines is often more qualified than from other sources, as users are actively seeking what you offer.

- *Credibility*: Top positions in search results convey a sense of credibility and authority to your brand.

- *Reduced Costs*: Unlike paid advertising (SEM, Search Engine Marketing), SEO, once correctly implemented, can bring traffic at zero cost.

SEO Fundamentals

1. *Keyword Research:*
   - *Identification:* Use tools like Google Keyword Planner, SEMrush, or Ahrefs to discover keywords relevant to your industry. Look for terms with good search volume and low competition.
   - *Demand Analysis*: Understand if the demand is transactional (purchase), informational (information), or navigational (navigating to a specific site).

2. *On-Page Optimization*:
   - *Titles and Tags:* Ensure your H1, H2 titles, and meta tags contain relevant keywords.
   - *Quality Content:* Content should be useful, relevant, and well-written. Google rewards original and valuable content.
   - *Friendly URLs:* URLs should be clear and contain keywords.

3. *Off-Page Optimization*:
   - *Link Building*: Building quality links from other websites to yours is crucial. This tells

Google your site is authoritative.

- *Social Mentions:* While social media does not directly pass link juice, it can drive traffic and mentions that indirectly help SEO.

4. *Technical SEO Techniques:*

- *Site Speed:* Faster sites are preferred by Google. Use tools like Google PageSpeed Insights to improve speed.

- *Mobile-Friendly*: With the increasing use of mobile devices, Google prioritizes mobile-optimized sites.

- *Site Structure:* Ensure the site is well-organized, with an XML sitemap and appropriate robots.txt file.

5. *Local SEO*:

- *Google My Business:* For local businesses, an optimized Google My Business profile is crucial.

- *Reviews and Citations*: Positive reviews and citations online can improve local visibility.

Advanced SEO Strategies

- *Content Marketing:* Create content that answers frequently asked questions or common problems in your industry. Blogs, guides, infographics can be very effective.

- *Voice SEO*: With the rise of voice assistants, optimize for natural and long-tail questions.

- *Video SEO*: Since YouTube is the second largest search engine, optimizing your videos with relevant keywords, detailed descriptions, and tags can expand your visibility.

- *EAT (Expertise, Authoritativeness, Trustworthiness)*: Google evaluates your expertise, authoritativeness, and trustworthiness in the field. Contribute to forums, write authoritative articles, and obtain certifications.

Monitoring and Analysis

- *Analysis Tools*: Use Google Analytics and Search Console to monitor your site's performance. These tools show which keywords work, which pages attract more traffic, and what improvements are needed.

- *Continuous Improvement*: SEO is not a one-time task. Strategies must be continuously updated based on search algorithm changes and market trends.

Conclusion

SEO is a complex but rewarding process. It requires time, resources, and a deep understanding of both techniques and current trends. However, with a well-thought-out strategy and consistent effort, SEO can transform a website from a mere online presence to a true reference point in its industry, increasing visibility, trust, and ultimately, business success.

5.2: Introduction to Search Engine Marketing (SEM)

Search Engine Marketing, commonly abbreviated as SEM, is a digital marketing strategy focused on enhancing a website's visibility on search engines through both free (SEO) and paid techniques (SEM in the strict sense, often associated with search engine advertising). While SEO aims to improve organic ranking, SEM includes paid campaigns to appear in sponsored results. This chapter will explore the fundamentals of SEM, focusing mainly on paid advertising campaigns, as SEO has been dealt with in detail previously.

Why is SEM Important?

- *Instant Visibility*: Unlike SEO, which can take time to show results, SEM campaigns can guarantee immediate visibility in the top search result positions.

- *Cost Control:* With SEM, you can set daily or monthly budgets and choose how much to pay per click (CPC - Cost Per Click), offering precise control over costs.

- *Precise Targeting:* You can segment the audience based on a variety of criteria, such as geographic location, interests, and online behavior, making the campaigns highly relevant to your target.

SEM Fundamentals

1. *SEM Platforms*:
   - *Google Ads*: Formerly Google AdWords, it's the best-known platform for search engine advertising. It offers a wide range of campaign options, including text ads, search ads, and Shopping campaigns.

   - *Bing Ads:* Although less used than Google, Bing can be effective for reaching a slightly different audience.

2. *SEM Campaign Structure:*

   - *Keyword Research*: Just like SEO, identifying the right keywords is crucial. However, here you can choose to bid on high-cost keywords if the return on investment (ROI) justifies it.

- *Ad Creation:* Text ads include titles, descriptions, and destination URLs. It's essential that ads are attractive and relevant to the selected keywords.

- *Match Types*: Google Ads campaigns allow you to choose how your keywords match user searches (exact, phrase, broad). This choice affects the relevance and cost of ads.

- *Budget Management*: You can set daily budgets and maximize ROI by setting competitive but advantageous CPCs.

3. *Effective SEM Strategies:*
- *SEO + SEM:* Combining SEO and SEM can maximize effectiveness. An SEO-optimized site can improve the performance of SEM campaigns, as optimized landing pages convert better.

- *Remarketing*: Using cookies to show your ads again to users who have already visited your site, increasing the likelihood of conversion.

- *A/B Testing:* Test different versions of ads and landing pages to see what works best in terms of click-through and conversion rates.

4. *Analysis and Optimization*:

- *Google Analytics*: By integrating Google Analytics with Google Ads, you can track conversions and see not just clicks, but also the actions users take after visiting your site.

- *Ad Quality:* Google assesses ad quality through the Quality Score, which impacts the cost of ads and where they appear. Improving relevance, user experience, and click-through rates can lower the cost per click.

Advantages and Disadvantages of SEM

- *Advantages:*
 - *Immediate*: Results are seen immediately.
 - *Scalability:* Campaigns can be easily scaled up or down based on performance.
 - *Measurability:* All aspects of campaigns are measurable, facilitating optimization.

- *Disadvantages:*
  - *Costs*: If not managed correctly, it can become expensive.
  - *Dependence*: Visibility depends on continuous spending on campaigns. Stopping spending can mean immediately losing visibility.

Advanced SEM Techniques

- *Automation*: Use Smart campaigns or automated campaigns to simplify management and automatically optimize campaigns based on collected data.

- *Display and Video:* Expand your presence not just in search results but also on websites and videos through display ad networks and TrueView.
- *Local SEM*: For local businesses, leverage location extensions to appear in searches with local intent.

Conclusion

SEM offers an opportunity for rapid and targeted visibility on search engines, where most people begin their online search. The key to success in SEM is a combination of a well-thought-out strategy, continuous data-driven optimization, and a deep understanding of how people interact with search engines. When executed correctly, SEM can be one of the most powerful tools in the digital marketer's toolkit, offering not just visibility but also tangible returns on investment.

5.3: Tools and Techniques
for Improving Ranking

Search engine ranking is an art that requires a combination of analysis, technique, and creativity. This chapter will explore various tools and techniques that can help improve your ranking, both through Search Engine Optimization (SEO) and Search Engine Marketing (SEM).

Essential SEO Tools

1. *Google Search Console:*
   - *Verification:* The first thing to do is verify your site with Google Search Console (GSC). This allows you to see how Google views your site, including indexing errors, search performance, and clicks.
   - *Tools*: GSC provides tools for sitemaps, internal link checking, and managing unindexed URLs.

2. *Google Analytics:*
   - *Tracking:* By integrating GA with GSC, you can track traffic, conversion rates, and user

behavior, allowing you to understand which pages perform better and where improvements are needed.

3. *Keyword Research Tools:*
   - *Google Keyword Planner*: Useful for finding new keywords, seeing their search volume, and estimating click costs if used in SEM campaigns.
   - *SEMrush, Ahrefs, Moz Keyword Explorer:* These offer deeper insights, including long-tail terms, competitor analysis, and content suggestions.

4. *Site Analysis Tools:*
   - *Google PageSpeed Insights*: Measures your site's speed for both desktop and mobile, offering advice to improve performance.
   - *Pingdom Website Speed Test:* Another tool to analyze site loading speed.

Advanced SEO Techniques

1. *Content Optimization:*
   - *On-Page SEO:* Ensure every page is optimized for one or more specific keywords.

This includes using H1, H2 tags, meta descriptions, and relevant content.

 - _EAT (Expertise, Authoritativeness, Trustworthiness):_ Create content that showcases your expertise, authoritativeness, and trustworthiness in your field.

2. _Link Building:_

 - _Guest Blogging:_ Write articles for other blogs in exchange for a backlink to your site.

 - _Broken Link Building_: Look for broken links on authoritative sites and contact the owners to suggest replacing them with links to your content.

3. _Technical SEO:_

 - _Site Architecture_: Ensure your site has a logical structure with SEO-friendly URLs.

 - _Mobile First:_ Optimize for mobile devices, as Google uses mobile-first indexing.

 - _HTTPS_: Ensure your site is secure with an SSL certificate.

4. _Local SEO:_

 - _Google My Business_: Manage and optimize your profile to appear in local searches.

- _Reviews and Citations_: Get positive reviews and cite your business online.

Tools and Techniques for SEM

1. _Google Ads_:
  - _Campaign Creation:_ Use Google Ads to create text, display, video, and shopping campaigns.
  - _Keyword Management_: Manage keywords to maximize campaign effectiveness, using appropriate match types.

2. _Bing Ads_:
  - _Alternative to Google_: Although less used, Bing offers good coverage, especially in specific markets.

3. _Analysis and Optimization Tools:_
  - _WordStream:_ Helps with PPC campaign management, keyword optimization, and competitor analysis.
  - _Optmyzr:_ Offers automation solutions for SEM, improving campaigns in real-time.

SEM Optimization Techniques

1. *A/B Testing:*
   - *Ads and Landing Pages:* Test variations of ads and landing pages to see which performs better in terms of CTR and conversions.

2. *Remarketing:*
   - *Search and Display Network:* Use remarketing to show ads to users who have already visited your site, increasing conversion likelihood.

3. Quality Score:
   - *Optimization:* Work on improving Google's Quality Score, which impacts the cost per click and ad position. This includes having relevant ads, good landing pages, and low bounce rates.

4. *Segmentation*:
   - *Advanced Targeting*: Use segmentations like demographics, interests, and behavior to make campaigns more relevant.

Monitoring and Adaptation

- *Reporting Tools:* Google Ads and Bing Ads

provide detailed reports. Use these to monitor performance and make real-time changes.

- *Continuous Adaptation*: The SEM world changes rapidly; stay updated with the latest trends and algorithm updates.

Conclusion

Improving ranking requires a combination of the right tools, an understanding of SEO and SEM techniques, and a continuous commitment to analysis and optimization. Whether you're looking to enhance your organic ranking or maximize the effectiveness of your paid campaigns, using the mentioned tools along with advanced techniques can make a difference in your site's visibility and, consequently, your business's success.

Chapter 6: Email Marketing: Building Relationships and Selling

6.1: Creating Email Lists and GDPR Compliance

In an era where digital marketing has become essential for business success, email marketing continues to stand out as one of the most effective tools for building customer relationships and increasing sales. However, creating email lists is not just about collecting addresses; it requires a well-thought-out strategy and strict compliance with current regulations, such as the GDPR (General Data Protection Regulation) of the European Union. This chapter will explore how to build effective email lists and ensure your practices comply with GDPR.

Creating Email Lists

1. *Consent Acquisition:*
   The foundation of any successful email list is explicit consent. Potential subscribers must be

informed about how their data will be used and must give their consent clearly. This process can occur through double opt-in, where the user signs up and then confirms their subscription via a verification email. This method not only ensures the person is genuinely interested but also helps maintain the list's quality.

2. _Segmentation_:

An email list is not monolithic; it consists of individuals with different preferences and buying behaviors. Segmenting your list by interests, purchase behavior, geography, etc., allows you to send more relevant emails, thereby increasing open and click-through rates. Tools like Mailchimp or Sendinblue offer advanced segmentation features.

3. _Quality vs. Quantity:_

It's tempting to aim for the largest number of subscribers possible, but the quality of the list is crucial. Better to have 10,000 highly interested subscribers than 100,000 indifferent ones. Quality translates into higher open rates, greater engagement, and ultimately, more sales.

4. *Subscription Sources:*

The sources from which email addresses come can vary: from your website, events, collaborations with other brands, to social media campaigns. Each source should be evaluated for the quality of subscribers it provides. For example, a popup on your website offering exclusive discounts might generate much more engaged subscribers than a purchased list.

5. *Feedback and Iteration:*

Email lists need to be dynamic. Use feedback, both positive and negative, to improve your offering. If subscribers complain about too many messages, consider reducing frequency. If emails aren't getting opened, it might be time to change the subject line or content.

GDPR Compliance

GDPR is one of the world's most stringent regulations for personal data protection. For those involved in email marketing, here are some key guidelines:

1. *Legal Basis for Data Processing:*

Every email sent must have a legal basis for processing personal data. Consent is the most common, but there are also other bases like legitimate interest, which must be justified in the specific case and cannot be used to send promotional emails without consent.

2. *Transparency:*

Subscribers must know exactly how and why their data is used. This means having a clear and accessible privacy policy that explains how data is collected, what data is collected, how it's used, and with whom it's shared.

3. *Rights of the Data Subject*:

GDPR grants individuals various rights, including the right to be forgotten, access to their data, rectification, data portability, and restriction of processing. Subscribers must be informed of these rights and there must be an easy mechanism to exercise them.

4. *Data Protection:*

Personal data must be protected against loss, unauthorized access, alteration, and destruction. This involves implementing adequate security measures like encryption and backup systems.

5. _Data Retention:_

Personal data must not be kept longer than necessary. This means when a subscriber unsubscribes, their personal data should be deleted or anonymized, unless necessary to comply with legal obligations or for explicit legitimate interest reasons.

6. _Breach Management:_

In case of a data breach, swift measures must be taken to inform competent authorities and, in some cases, the individuals involved. This implies having a breach response plan ready.

7. _Accountability and Privacy by Design_:

Accountability requires businesses to demonstrate GDPR compliance. Privacy by Design means data protection must be integrated into the design and management of all business processes.

Conclusion

Building an effective email list is as much an art as it is a science, requiring a balance between acquisition and quality, and careful data management to comply with GDPR. Companies that succeed in this not only build stronger relationships with customers but also a reputation for reliability and respect for privacy, essential elements in the modern world of digital marketing. Remember, the key to success is not just in the number of email addresses you have, but in the quality of the interactions you can have with each one.

6.2: Writing Emails That Convert

Email marketing remains one of the most powerful tools in a marketer's toolkit for a fundamental reason: its ability to convert. However, not all emails are created equal; some manage to generate actions, while others end up in the trash. In this chapter, we'll explore strategies for writing emails that not only capture attention but also push readers to take the desired action, whether it's making a purchase, signing up for a webinar, or simply opening a new link.

Essential Elements of a Converting Email

1. *Email Subject Line:*
  The subject line is the first impression. It should be intriguing but not misleading. Here are some strategies:
  - *Personalization:* Including the recipient's name or personal references increases open rates.
  - *Questions and Curiosity*: Creating a sense of curiosity ("Did you forget something?").
  - *Urgency:* Words like "Last Day," "Special Offer," "Deadline" can prompt action.
  - *Clarity:* Avoid being too cryptic; the subject line should give a good indication of the content.

2. *Email Structure:*
  - *Header:* A brief introduction or a captivating image. Consider using a visual preview.

- *Email Body:* Break content into short sections. Use bold text, bullet points, and images to maintain interest.

- *Call to Action (CTA):* Clear, visible, and single CTAs are more effective. Use color contrast to make them stand out.

3. *Quality Content:*

- *Relevance*: The content must be relevant to the recipient. Using segmentation and personalization is crucial.

- *Value*: Offer something of value, whether it's a promotion, educational content, or an exclusive preview.

- *Conversational Style:* Write as you speak. Emails should feel like a direct conversation with the recipient.

4. *Proof of Credibility*:

Include reviews, testimonials, or statistics that demonstrate the value of your product or service. This increases trust.

5. *Design and Images:*

- *Mobile-Friendly*: Most emails are read on mobile devices. Ensure the design is responsive.

- *Images:* Use high-quality images, but not excessively. Emails with images have higher open rates, but balance is key.

Copywriting Techniques for Email

1. *Storytelling:*
Stories engage. Tell a story that connects your product or service to the recipient's problem or desire. For example, describe how a product changed someone's life.

2. *Scarcity Principle*:
Creating a sense of scarcity ("Only 10 items left") or urgency ("Offer valid until midnight") can prompt action.

3. *Social Proof:*
Showing that other people approve or use your product (testimonials, user numbers, etc.) can positively influence.

4. *Rhetorical Questions:*
Using questions like "Have you ever wondered how...?" can stimulate critical thinking and the desire to discover more.

5. *Emotional Language:*
Emotions drive decisions. Use words that evoke specific feelings like joy, curiosity, or anxiety.

Optimization and Testing

1. *A/B Testing*:
Test different versions of the email to see which performs better. You might test the subject line, CTA, layout, or copy.

2. *Data Analysis*:
Monitor metrics like open rates, clicks, conversions. These data will tell you what works and what doesn't.

3. *Feedback Loop:*
Use subscriber feedback to improve. If many unsubscribe, it might be a sign that the content is not appreciated.

4. *Timing:*
The time and day of sending can have a significant impact. Test different times to see

when your audience is most receptive.

Specific Strategies for Conversions

1. *Welcome Email:*
The first email should be welcoming, offer immediate value (discount, free content), and set expectations for future communications.

2. *Cart Abandonment Email:*
Use a series of emails gently reminding users to complete their purchase, perhaps offering a discount or incentive.

3. *Frequency Email:*
Not just promotions, but emails that inform about news, updates, or simply keep in touch.

4. *Re-engagement Email:*
If a customer hasn't interacted for a while, an email that welcomes them back and invites them to return with a special offer can be effective.

5. *Upsell and Cross-sell Email:*
Suggesting complementary or higher-tier

products can increase the average order value.

Conclusion

Writing emails that convert is a refined art that combines psychology, technique, and data. The key is to understand your audience, offer value, and create a sense of urgency or exclusivity. Remember, each email is an opportunity to build or strengthen a relationship, not just to sell. With the right strategies, emails can become one of the most profitable channels in your marketing arsenal.

6.3: Automation and Personalization
of Email Campaigns

Automation and personalization have become the buzzwords of modern email marketing. These two elements not only make email campaigns more efficient but also more effective, improving engagement and conversions. In this chapter, we will explore how to integrate automation and personalization into your email marketing strategies to maximize impact and build stronger relationships with your subscribers.

The Importance of Automation

1. *Efficiency:*
   Automation allows you to schedule email sends based on specific triggers such as sign-ups, cart abandonment, or a customer's birthday. This means you can maintain a steady flow of communications without the need to manually send each email.

2. *Scalability:*
   As your subscriber list grows, managing

communications manually becomes unfeasible. Automation enables scalability without compromising the quality or timeliness of emails.

3. _Consistency_:

It ensures that every subscriber receives the right information or offers at the right time, maintaining a high-quality user experience.

Automation Strategies

1. _Welcome Emails:_

First impressions are crucial. An automated welcome series can include an introduction to the brand, a special offer, and information on how subscribers can expect to interact with you.

2. _Cart Abandonment Emails:_

When a customer leaves your site without completing a purchase, a gentle reminder email can recover sales.

3. _Re-engagement Emails:_

For subscribers who haven't interacted for a

while, a series of emails inviting them back with exclusive offers or content.

4. *Behavior-Based Emails:*

Use automation to send emails based on how users interact with your site or app, such as product recommendations based on past purchases.

5. *Frequency Management:*

Automation algorithms can adjust the frequency of emails based on subscriber engagement, avoiding overload and maintaining interest.

The Art of Personalization

1. *Name and Personal Data:*

Including the recipient's name or personal references (like their city) increases open rates. However, ensure the data is accurate and used respectfully.

2. *Segmentation:*

Divide your subscriber list into segments based on interests, purchase behavior, or other relevant variables. This allows for sending highly relevant content.

3. *Dynamic Content:*

Use dynamic content that changes based on who is receiving the email, like recommended products or articles based on past interests.

4. *Behavioral Personalization:*

Based on previous behaviors, like pages visited or products viewed, offer content or deals that reflect these interests.

5. *Feedback and Preferences:*

Encourage subscribers to provide feedback or select content preferences, allowing you to send more relevant emails.

Integration of Automation and Personalization

1. *Automated Workflows:*

Create workflows that include personalization points. For example, a birthday email that not only acknowledges the special date but also offers a discount on a product the subscriber recently viewed.

2. *Dynamic Triggers:*
Use triggers that not only start an email series but can also alter the path based on subscriber actions or inactions.

3. *Customized A/B Testing:*
While automation can send emails, testing can determine which personalized version works best for each audience segment.

4. *Automated Feedback*:
Implement systems that automatically collect feedback and use it to improve future personalization.

Challenges and Considerations

1. *Balancing Personalization and Privacy:*
While personalization is powerful, it's crucial to respect data protection laws and ensure personal data is used ethically.

2. *Email Overload:*
Even though automation can improve efficiency, sending too many emails can lead

to unsubscribes. Find a balance and allow subscribers to choose their frequency.

3. *Technology and Integration:*
Use automation tools that integrate well with other platforms (CRM, e-commerce, analytics) for consistency in messaging and user experience.

4. *Measuring Effectiveness:*
Continuously monitor the effectiveness of your automation and personalization strategies. Use KPIs like open rates, click-through rates, and conversions to optimize continuously.

Conclusion

Automation and personalization are not just trends; they are imperatives for email marketing success in an increasingly digital world. While automation allows you to scale and maintain an efficient operation, personalization ensures each message is relevant and engaging. By combining these strategies, you can build stronger relationships with your subscribers, increase sales, and create a significant competitive advantage.

Remember, the heart of email marketing is the relationship, and automation and personalization are the tools that allow you to maintain and enhance these relationships effectively and at scale.

Chapter 7:

Marketing through Data Analytics:

How to Use Data to Your Advantage

7.1: Introduction to Data Analytics in Marketing

In the modern marketing world, Data Analytics has become an indispensable tool for any industry professional. But what exactly are Data Analytics, and why are they so critical?

What is Data Analytics?

Data Analytics refers to the process of examining, cleaning, transforming, and modeling data to uncover useful information, insights, and support strategic decision-making. In a marketing context, this means collecting and analyzing data from various sources to better understand consumer behavior, improve ad campaigns, optimize sales strategies, and much more.

Types of Data in Marketing

1. *Demographic Data*: Age, gender, income, education level, occupation, etc. These data help segment the market into specific groups for better targeting campaigns.

2. *Behavioral Data:* Includes information on how consumers interact with the brand, which products they purchase, how much time they spend on a website, which pages they visit, and even interactions on social platforms.

3. *Psychographic Data*: Interests, opinions, attitudes, values. These data provide a deeper insight into the personality and preferences of consumers.

4. *Contextual Data: I*nformation about the

location, time, and circumstances in which consumers interact with a company. For example, seasonal sales, special promotions, or local events can influence purchasing behavior.

Why are Data Analytics Fundamental?

- *Personalization*: Data Analytics allow for tailoring messages and offers so they resonate with individual consumers. Personalization increases the relevance of the message, improving engagement and conversions.
- *Campaign Optimization:* By analyzing past campaign performance data, companies can understand what worked and what didn't, continuously improving their strategies.

- *Trend Prediction:* Through predictive analytics, companies can anticipate changes in consumer behavior, adapting strategies before trends fully materialize.

- *Advanced Segmentation:* Data allows for more precise market segmentation, identifying niches that might not be obvious at first glance. This can lead to highly targeted campaigns that generate higher ROI.

- *Operational Efficiency:* Detailed data on costs, profits, and campaign efficiency help reduce waste, optimizing resource use.

- *Real-Time Feedback:* Thanks to Data Analytics, companies can monitor the effectiveness of their strategies in real-time, making immediate adjustments to maximize results.

Challenges in Data Analytics for Marketing
Despite the benefits, implementing Data Analytics presents challenges:

- *Data Quality:* Data must be accurate and clean. Incorrect or incomplete data can lead to wrong conclusions.

- *Privacy and Regulations*: With GDPR, CCPA, and other regulations, managing personal data requires careful handling to avoid privacy breaches and legal penalties.

- *Technical Competence:* Analyzing data

requires specific skills in statistics, programming, and data analysis tools. Not all companies have access to staff with these skills.

- *System Integration:* Many companies use different tools to collect data. Integrating this data cohesively can be complex.

Tools Used

The market offers a wide range of tools for data analysis in marketing:

- *Google Analytics:* Essential for analyzing web traffic, user behavior, and traffic sources.

- *CRM (Customer Relationship Management) Systems*: Like Salesforce, HubSpot, which not only manage customer relationships but also track and analyze interactions.

- *Business Intelligence Tools*: Such as Tableau or Power BI, which offer interactive data visualizations for more intuitive analysis.

- *Social Media Analytics Tools*: To monitor engagement, sentiment, and interactions on social media.

- *Machine Learning and AI*: Used for predictive analytics and to personalize marketing experiences at scale.

Conclusion

Data Analytics in marketing are not just a competitive advantage; they have become a requirement to remain relevant in an increasingly competitive and saturated market. The ability to collect, analyze, and act on this data makes the difference between successful and failed campaigns. As technology progresses, the importance of Data Analytics will continue to grow, making it essential for every marketer to understand and leverage these tools. The key is not just collecting data but transforming it into actions that create value for the company and the customer.

7.2: Tools and Software in Data Analytics for Marketing

In the marketing sector, the use of Data Analytics tools and software is crucial for effectively collecting, analyzing, and interpreting data. These tools not only enhance the understanding of consumer behavior but also make it possible to optimize marketing strategies. Below, we explore some of the most popular and powerful tools available to marketers.

Google Analytics

Google Analytics is probably the most well-known and widely used web analytics tool. Here are some of its key features:

- *Data Collection:* Tracks your website traffic, monitoring visits, pages viewed, session duration, and much more.

- *Behavior Analysis:* Provides details on how users interact with your site, indicating which pages are most popular and where users exit (bounce rate).

- *Conversion Funnel*: Helps visualize the user path towards specific goals, like a purchase or sign-up.

- *Segmentation*: Allows for segmenting traffic to better understand performance with different user groups.

- *Real-Time Reports*: Offers real-time data on who is visiting the site now, useful for events or live campaigns.

SEMrush

SEMrush is a powerful tool for Search Engine Optimization (SEO) and competitive analysis:

- *SEO Toolkit:* Offers detailed analysis on on-page and off-page SEO, keyword tracking, and suggestions to improve search engine rankings.

- *Competitive Analysis:* Scans competitors' sites to understand their SEO strategies, which keywords they use, and their link building campaigns.

- *Keyword Research:* Identifies high-volume, low-competition keywords, optimizing SEO strategy.

- *Backlink Analysis:* Examines incoming links to your site and competitors', providing insights to improve site authority.

- *Advertising Research*: Provides insights into competitors' PPC (Pay Per Click) campaigns, useful information for optimizing your campaigns.

HubSpot

HubSpot is a CRM (Customer Relationship Management) that includes powerful marketing analytics tools:

- *Marketing Automation*: Automates email marketing, social media, and other marketing activities, analyzing campaign effectiveness.

- *Lead Scoring:* Helps identify which leads are most likely to become customers, based on behaviors and demographic data.

- *Marketing Websites:* Creates marketing-optimized websites, with integrated analytics and SEO tools.

- *Contact Analysis:* Provides detailed reports on how contacts interact with your brand across different channels.

Tableau

Tableau is a Business Intelligence (BI) tool that turns data into interactive visualizations:

- *Interactive Dashboards*: Creates dashboards that allow for real-time data visualization and analysis, facilitating decision-making.

- *Data Analysis:* Supports data analysis from both internal and external sources, integrating with databases, Google Analytics, and other services.

- *Big Data Analytics*: Capable of handling large volumes of data, useful for companies with large datasets to analyze.

- *Sharing and Collaboration:* Facilitates data sharing and collaboration, allowing teams to work together on analytics projects.

Hootsuite

Hootsuite is a social media management tool that also offers analytics features:

- *Social Media Analytics:* Monitors engagement, followers, and other metrics on social platforms, offering detailed reports.

- *Mention Monitoring:* Detects when your brand is mentioned, allowing for timely responses and sentiment monitoring.

- *Scheduled Publishing*: Schedules posts in

advance and analyzes each post's performance to optimize the editorial calendar.

- *Competitive Analysis*: Compares social media performance with competitors to improve your strategy.

Power BI

Microsoft's Power BI is another potent Business Intelligence tool:

- *Multi-source Connection*: Can connect to a wide range of data sources, including ERP, CRM, and business databases to create a unified view.

- *Advanced Analytics*: Offers tools for predictive analytics and machine learning, helping to forecast future market trends.

- *Interactive Visualizations:* Like Tableau, allows for creating dynamic and interactive reports that enhance data understanding and interpretation.

- _Accessibility:_ Can be used by marketing teams without advanced data analysis skills, thanks to an intuitive interface.

Conclusion

The tools mentioned above offer a wide range of functionalities that allow marketers to collect, analyze, and interpret data in increasingly sophisticated ways. The choice of tool depends on the specific needs of your marketing project, available budget, and the technical competence of your team. By integrating these tools into marketing strategies, companies can make data-driven decisions, improving campaign effectiveness and customer engagement. The key to success is using these tools not just as mere data collectors but as catalysts for growth and innovation in your industry.

7.3: Interpreting Data:

How to Use Data to Optimize Marketing Campaigns

Interpreting the data collected is one of the most crucial stages in the process of Data Analytics in marketing. It's not enough just to collect data; it's vital to know how to read, analyze, and transform it into strategic actions that enhance engagement, optimize marketing campaigns, and increase conversions. This chapter will explore strategies and methodologies for effectively interpreting data for marketing strategies.

Traffic Data Analysis

- *Traffic Sources:* Understanding where traffic comes from (organic, direct, referral, social media, PPC campaigns) is essential for better resource allocation. If social media traffic Is high but conversions are low, it might indicate issues with targeting or traffic quality.

- *User Behavior:* Analyzing the user journey on the site (conversion funnel) shows where users drop off in the purchasing process. This can point to usability or content issues.

Audience Segmentation

- *Demographics and Psychographics:* Use data to segment the audience by age, gender, interests, and behavior. This allows for personalized offers and messaging, increasing relevance and effectiveness.

- *Analysis of Past Behavior*: Examine previous purchases and interactions to predict future preferences and lean towards behavior-based marketing.

Campaign Optimization

- *Campaign Performance*: Compare the performance of different campaigns, identifying what works (headlines, creatives, offers, CTAs). For example, if an email campaign with a temporary promotion has a higher open and conversion rate, it might indicate a preference for immediate offers.

- *A/B Testing:* Use data to conduct A/B tests on elements like the CTA button color, message content, or landing page layout to see which version performs better.

Improving Engagement

- *Time on Site and Pages Viewed*: An increase in time spent and pages viewed might indicate engaging content. However, if these metrics are high but conversions are low, there might be an issue in the sales funnel.

- *Social Media Engagement:* Analyze likes, comments, shares to understand which types of content generate more interaction. This can guide future content creation.

Increasing Conversions

- *Conversion Funnel:* Each step of the funnel must be analyzed. If the dropout rate is high at a specific point, focus efforts there. It might be necessary to improve site speed, simplify the buying process, or offer incentives.

- *Conversion Analysis:* Examine which campaigns, channels, and content generate more conversions to understand where to invest more. If a social channel has a high conversion rate, it might be worth increasing the budget for that channel.

Using Advanced Metrics

- *LTV (Lifetime Value):* Calculating customer lifetime value helps understand how much it's worth investing in each customer. Loyalty and upselling strategies can be optimized based on this data.

- *ROI (Return on Investment):* Analyze the ROI of each campaign to see which yields the highest return and where there's room for improvement. A negative ROI can indicate that the chosen strategies or channels are not optimal.

- *CAC (Customer Acquisition Cost):* It's important to know how much it costs to acquire a new customer. If CAC is high compared to LTV, acquisition strategies might need reviewing.

Predictive Tools and Machine Learning

- *Predictive Analysis*: Use predictive models to forecast future consumer behavior or identify the most promising leads. These models can suggest ideal times for promotions based on past purchase cycles.
- *Machine Learning*: Machine learning algorithms can optimize campaigns in real-time, for example, by modifying offers or content based on engagement or cart abandonment.

Implementing Discoveries

- *Feedback Loop:* Create a continuous cycle of data collection, analysis, and action. Every discovery should lead to a change in strategy or tactics.

- *Internal Communication*: Ensure that the analysis results are clearly communicated to marketing, sales, and product development teams to provide a unified vision and coordinated action.

Conclusion

Interpreting data in marketing isn't just about numbers; it's the art of turning those numbers into stories that narrate consumer behavior. Every piece of data collected is a puzzle piece that, when assembled, provides a clear picture of how the audience interacts with the brand. The key to continuous campaign optimization, increased engagement, and conversions lies in the ability to listen to what the data tells and act accordingly. With the advent of advanced technologies like predictive analytics and machine learning, this ability to interpret and act on data becomes increasingly critical for success in modern marketing.

7.4: A/B Testing: Methodologies for Testing Different Campaign Variants and Understanding What Works Best

A/B Testing is one of the most powerful methodologies in marketing and campaign optimization, allowing marketers to compare two versions of the same campaign, webpage, or design element to determine which performs better. This process helps make data-driven decisions, reducing assumptions and increasing the likelihood of marketing strategy success. Let's explore how it works, which methodologies to use, and how to interpret the results.

What is A/B Testing?

A/B Testing involves presenting two versions (A and B) of a specific element (like an email, landing page, or CTA) to two similar groups of users. Version A is generally the current or control version, while B represents the modified variant. The performance of these variants is monitored and compared to determine which version yields better results, which could be conversion rates, click-through rates, email open rates, etc.

A/B Testing Methodologies

1. *Goal Definition:* First, clarify what you want to test and improve. Goals might include increasing conversion rates, improving email open rates, or boosting social media engagement.

2. *Choosing the Variable to Test:* Decide which campaign element you want to test. It could be the color of a button, the text of a CTA, the structure of a landing page, or even the time of an email send.

3. *Creating Variants*: Develop versions A and B, ensuring the difference between them is significant enough to potentially affect user behavior. For example, if testing an email, variants might include different subjects, images, or layouts.

4. *Audience Segmentation:* Divide your audience into two random groups, ensuring both are representative of your target

audience in terms of size, demographics, and past behavior.

5. *Test Execution:* Launch both versions simultaneously. This is crucial to avoid external changes (like news events or seasonal variations) affecting results.

6. *Data Collection and Analysis*: Monitor relevant metrics. Use tools like Google Analytics, Optimizely, or HubSpot to collect data in real-time or upon test completion.

7. *Statistical Analysis:* To determine if one variant outperforms the other, statistical analysis is necessary. This can be done with significance tests (like the Z-test or chi-square test) to understand if the observed difference is due to chance or is significant.

8. *Decision and Implementation*: If variant B shows statistically better performance, implement that version permanently. If variant A wins, it might indicate further tests or new ideas are needed.

Examples of A/B Testing

- *Email Marketing:* Testing send time, email subject, or promotional offer to see which combination has the highest open rate.

- *Landing Pages:* Varying design, CTA, or text content to understand which layout or message converts more visitors.

- *Checkout Pages:* Testing the order of form fields, offering free shipping, or the design of the "Buy" button to reduce cart abandonment.

- *Social Media Ads:* Trying different images, copy, or audience targeting to see which ad has the best engagement or lowest cost per conversion.

Best Practices for Effective A/B Testing

- *Test Duration*: Ensure the test runs long enough to gather significant data but not so long that the results become outdated.

- *Sample Size:* A sufficiently large sample is crucial for statistically significant results. Online sample calculators can help determine the appropriate size.

- *One Variable at a Time:* To isolate the effect of a change, only alter one element per test. Testing too many variables simultaneously can muddle results.

- *Test Stability:* Keep all other external variables stable that might influence results, like other active campaigns or site changes.

- *Continuous Analysis*: Even after implementing changes, continue monitoring to ensure performance remains stable.

Interpreting Results

Not all observed differences are significant. It's important to:
- *Evaluate Statistical Significance:* A slight improvement might not be significant if it doesn't surpass the statistical significance threshold.

- *Consider Context:* Even if a variant performs better, assess if the improvement justifies the change in terms of costs and time.

- *Iteration:* A/B testing should be an ongoing process. Even after finding a winning version, keep testing new ideas for further improvements.

Conclusion

A/B testing is a scientific method for optimizing marketing strategies, relying on empirical evidence rather than intuition or personal preferences. Through a systematic and iterative approach, companies can continuously improve their campaigns, enhancing the effectiveness of marketing strategies and, consequently, commercial outcomes. The key is not to view A/B testing as a one-off event but as a practice integrated into the company's culture of continuous improvement.

7.5: Forecasting and Optimization:

Using Data to Predict Trends and Optimize Future Strategies

The marketing world is constantly evolving, and the ability to predict trends and optimize strategies based on historical and real-time data has become an essential skill. In this chapter, we will explore how data analytics techniques can be used to forecast market trends and optimize future marketing strategies.

1. Data Collection and Cleaning

The first critical phase is data collection and cleaning. Data can come from various sources: sales, social media, customer feedback, website interactions, and many others. It's vital to have a robust system for data collection that can efficiently handle massive volumes of information.

- *Collection:* Use tools like Google Analytics, CRM, and social media platforms to gather data.

- *Cleaning:* Remove or correct erroneous, duplicate, or incomplete data. This process is crucial to ensure subsequent analysis is accurate.

2. Exploratory Data Analysis (EDA)

EDA is the process of analyzing data to discover patterns, anomalies, test hypotheses, and develop insights. This step is crucial to understand the nature of data and identify the most relevant variables.

- *Visualization:* Create charts and diagrams to visualize trends and correlations.
- *Descriptive Statistics*: Calculate means, medians, standard deviations to understand data distribution.

3. Predictive Models

Once the data is cleaned and understood, predictive models can be built. These models use machine learning algorithms to make predictions based on historical data.

- *Regression:* Used to predict numerical values, like sales volume.
- *Classification*: Suitable for predicting categories, such as the likelihood of a customer purchasing a product.
- *Time Series:* Excellent for predicting variables that change over time, like seasonal sales.

4. Trend Forecasting

Forecasting market trends is one of the most powerful uses of data. This can include:

- *Market Trends:* Using data to predict which products will be popular in the future.
- *Consumer Behavior*: Analyzing behavioral data to predict changes in consumer preferences.
- *External Events:* Considering the impact of events like holidays, economic crises, or legislative changes.

5. Strategy Optimization

Optimization is the process of improving

performance based on forecasts and data analysis.

- *A/B Testing:* Trying different campaign versions to see which performs better.
- *Segmentation*: Using data to segment the audience into more homogeneous groups to personalize offers.
- *Automation:* Implementing automated marketing campaigns that adapt in real-time to data changes.

6. Closed-Loop Feedback

A closed-loop feedback system involves using the data collected during and after a campaign to inform and refine future strategies.

- *Real-Time Monitoring:* Analyzing campaign results as they develop.
- *Continuous Adaptation:* Modifying ongoing campaigns based on real-time performance data.

7. Ethics and Privacy

With the intensive use of data, ethical and

legal considerations are crucial.

- *Data Protection*: Ensuring all data collection and use practices comply with privacy regulations like GDPR.
- *Transparency:* Being transparent with customers about how their data is used.

8. Tools and Technologies

To effectively implement data analytics strategies in marketing, it's important to know and use the appropriate tools:

- *Analytics Platforms:* Google Analytics, Adobe Analytics, Tableau.
- *Machine Learning*: Using platforms like TensorFlow or scikit-learn.
- *Big Data:* Tools like Hadoop or Spark for handling large data volumes.

9. Case Study: Email Marketing Campaign Optimization

A practical example can help clarify the application of these concepts. Suppose we want to optimize an email marketing campaign:

- *Data Analysis:* Identify times of the day and week when emails have the highest open rates.
- *Predictive Models*: Create a model to predict which type of content (promotions, news, updates) is most likely to generate a click.
- *Implementation*: Use this data to segment the audience and send personalized emails.
- *Feedback:* Monitor responses and update the forecasting model with new data.

Conclusion

Using data to predict trends and optimize future strategies is not just a competitive advantage but a necessity in the modern marketing landscape. The ability to collect, analyze, and interpret data, combined with predictive modeling, provides a clear picture of how the market will move and allows for proactive adaptation. The key is maintaining an iterative approach, continuously refining strategies based on new available data, always respecting ethics and privacy. With the advent of machine learning and big data technologies, this practice will become increasingly crucial for the success of marketing campaigns.

Chapter 8:
Visual and Graphic Marketing:

Creating a Visual Impact

8.1: Importance of Visual Marketing:

Why Images, Videos, and Infographics Have Become So Crucial in Modern Marketing

In an era where attention is the most valuable commodity, visual marketing emerges as one of the most potent tools to capture and retain audience interest. Images, videos, and infographics not only make content more engaging but communicate messages quickly and effectively. This chapter explores the importance of visual marketing and how these forms of communication have revolutionized how brands interact with consumers.

1. Visual Psychology: Why It Works

The human brain is wired to respond visually. Studies show that 80% of the information

139

received by the brain is visual, and the brain can process images up to 60,000 times faster than text. This processing speed makes visual marketing particularly effective:

- *Attention:* Images and videos grab attention much faster than text. On a social feed, users will notice posts with captivating images first.
- *Memory:* Visual information is remembered more easily and for longer. For example, videos or infographics can convey complex business concepts in a memorable way.

2. Quick and Effective Communication

In a world where attention is fragmented, communicating quickly is essential. Visual marketing allows conveying complex messages concisely:

- *Infographics*: Great for presenting data and statistics in a clear, visually engaging way. They can transform a series of numbers into an understandable story.
- *Videos:* Can tell a brand story, show products in action, or educate on a topic within minutes, keeping the audience interested.

3. Engagement and Interaction

Visual content does more than just grab attention; it increases interaction:

- *Social Media:* Social platforms are dominated by visual content. Posts with images or videos tend to receive more likes, comments, and shares than text-only posts.
- *User-Generated Content*: Encouraging customers to create and share visual content increases engagement and trust in the brand.

4. Market Differentiation

In a saturated market, differentiation is crucial. Visual marketing offers the chance to create a unique visual identity:

- *Brand Identity*: Images and videos can reinforce brand identity, creating a consistent visual experience across all customer touchpoints.

- *Graphic Style*: A distinctive design can make a brand immediately recognizable, even without a logo.

5. Emerging Technologies and Visual Marketing

The advent of new technologies has expanded the possibilities of visual marketing:

- *Augmented Reality (AR) and Virtual Reality (VR)*: These technologies offer immersive experiences, ideal for experiential marketing.
- *360° Video:* Allows consumers to explore products or environments from every angle, enhancing interaction.

6. SEO and Visual Marketing

Visual marketing isn't just about aesthetics; it also significantly impacts search engine optimization:

- *Visual SEO:* Optimized images with keywords, alt text, and meta descriptions can improve visibility in search results.

- *Pinterest and Google Images:* These visual search engines are gaining popularity, offering unique opportunities for marketing through images.

7. Success Stories

- *Instagram:* It has become a successful platform due to its focus on images and videos. Brands like Nike use Instagram for visual campaigns that tell stories through high-quality images.
- *GoPro:* Built an entire brand around the concept of "capturing the moment." Their marketing campaigns are centered on impressive videos showcasing product use in extreme situations.

8. Tools for Visual Marketing

To effectively implement visual marketing, it's important to know and use the right tools:

- *Canva:* Perfect for creating infographics, posters, and social posts without advanced graphic skills.

- *Adobe Creative Suite:* Professional tools like Photoshop and Premiere Pro for advanced image and video editing.
- *Video Maker:* Apps like InShot or Vidnami for creating high-quality videos.

9. Practical Tips for Implementation

- *Visual Consistency:* Maintain a consistent style and theme across all platforms.
- *Quality Over Quantity*: Better to have fewer high-quality visual contents than many low-quality ones.
- *Storytelling:* Use images and videos to tell a story that resonates with the target audience.

Conclusion

Visual marketing is not just a trend; it's a necessity driven by the evolution of consumer behaviors and available technologies. Images, videos, and infographics have become essential tools to communicate effectively, engage audiences, and stand out in a crowded market. For those looking to make a visual impact, the importance of integrating these forms of marketing into one's arsenal is clear. Not only do they enhance campaign effectiveness, but they also help build an emotional and lasting connection with the audience, making visual marketing an indispensable component of modern success.

8.2: Creation Tools:

Introduction to Tools like Adobe Photoshop, Canva, or Open Source Software for Creating Visual Content

The creation of visual content has become an essential skill for anyone looking to excel in modern marketing. Whether it's images for social media, infographics to present data, or videos for advertising campaigns, familiarity with visual creation tools is crucial. In this chapter, we'll explore some of the most popular visual creation tools, analyzing their features, advantages, and how they can be used to create impactful content.

1. Adobe Photoshop

Adobe Photoshop is one of the most powerful and versatile photographic editing tools available. It has long been the software of choice for professionals in design, photography, and marketing.

- Functionality: Photoshop offers a broad range of tools for image editing, from photo retouching to digital painting. It can be used to manipulate images, create graphics, and even animations.

- Use in Marketing:

  - Photo Retouching: Enhance product images, remove imperfections, and create complex compositions.

  - Banner and Poster Design: Create high-quality promotional material.

  - Infographics: Though less common, can be used to create complex sections of infographics.

- Advantages:

  - Power and Flexibility: Offers almost infinite control over images.

  - Adobe Ecosystem: Integrates well with other Adobe products like Illustrator and Premiere Pro.

- *Challenges:*
  - *Learning Curve*: Can be complex for beginners.
  - *Cost:* Requires a monthly or annual subscription.

2. Canva

Canva has become the go-to for many marketers seeking user-friendly tools to create visual content without needing advanced design skills.

- *Functionality:* Canva provides an intuitive interface with pre-designed templates for virtually every type of visual content imaginable, from social media posts to presentations, flyers, and even videos.

- *Use in Marketing:*
  - *Social Media Posts*: Designed to be easy to use, it's perfect for quick, high-quality posts.
  - *Promotional Material:* Easily create brochures, business cards, and posters.
  - *Infographics*: With a wide selection of templates, it's excellent for creating infographics.

- *Advantages:*
  - *Simplicity*: Drag-and-drop interface and pre-set templates.
  - *Accessibility*: Free version with premium options for advanced features.
  - *Collaboration:* Real-time collaboration features.
- *Challenges:*
  - *Creative Limitations*: Less flexible for complex or custom design work.

3. Adobe Illustrator

While less used for daily visual marketing compared to Photoshop, Illustrator is essential for creating vector graphics.

- *Functionality:* Specialized in vector graphics, ideal for logos, icons, illustrations, and anything that requires scalability without quality loss.

- *Use in Marketing:*
  - *Logo Design:* Create logos that can be resized without quality loss.
  - *Illustrations*: Use for creating images that require precise details and clean lines.
  - *Graphic Elements:* Produce icons, borders,

and ornaments for promotional material.

- *Advantages:*
  - *Scalability:* Vector designs that can be enlarged infinitely.
  - *Precision*: Advanced tools for precise drawing.

- *Challenges:*
  - *Complexity*: More difficult to learn than Canva.
  - *Cost:* Part of Adobe Creative Cloud subscription.

4. Open Source Software

For those looking for cost-effective alternatives, there are numerous open-source tools that offer similar functionalities, albeit with different limitations.

- *GIMP (GNU Image Manipulation Program):*
  - *Functionality:* Similar to Photoshop, offers tools for raster image editing.
  - *Advantages:* Free and open source, supported by an active community.
  - *Challenges:* Less intuitive interface and fewer features than Photoshop.

- *Inkscape:*
  - *Functionality:* Comparable to Adobe Illustrator, specialized in vector graphics.
  - *Advantages:* Free and powerful for vector drawing.
  - *Challenges:* Fewer advanced options and plugins than Illustrator.

5. Video and Animation Tools

- *DaVinci Resolve*:
  - *Functionality:* Professional video editing and color grading.
  - *Advantages*: Free for the basic version, with advanced options available for purchase.
- *Blender:*
  - *Functionality:* 3D creation, animations, and compositing.
  - *Advantages:* Open source, powerful for 3D creations and animations.
  - *Challenges*: Steep learning curve for beginners.

Conclusion

Choosing the right tool for creating visual content depends on specific needs, budget, and design skill level. Adobe Photoshop and Illustrator offer flexibility and power for complex work, while Canva is ideal for a quick, user-friendly approach. Open-source tools like GIMP and Inkscape are excellent for those seeking free solutions without too much compromise on quality. Regardless of the tool chosen, mastering the basics is key to fully leveraging the potential of visual marketing, transforming ideas into images that capture attention and tell a story.

8.3: Design Basics:

Fundamental Principles of Graphic Design Applied to Online Marketing

Success in online marketing doesn't just depend on the strength of the message but also, and perhaps most importantly, on its visual presentation. In the digital world, where user attention is fragmented and competition is fierce, graphic design becomes a crucial element for capturing and maintaining audience interest. This chapter will explore the fundamental principles of graphic design that are essential for creating effective visual content in online marketing: contrast, consistency, and visual hierarchy.

Contrast

Contrast is one of the most powerful tools in design. It refers to the difference between visual elements that makes one distinguishable from another. In online marketing, contrast can be used in various ways:

- *Color:* Use complementary or highly contrasting colors (like black and white, red and green) to highlight key elements such as call-to-actions (CTAs), headlines, or logos. This helps guide the user's eye to focal points.

- *Size:* Varying the size of elements to create a sense of importance. For example, a large headline on a webpage catches attention compared to smaller text.

- *Tone:* Combining light and dark tones to create depth and interest. Text on a dark background with light outlines or vice versa.

- *Typography:* Using fonts from different families or styles (serif, sans-serif, italic) to distinguish sections or types of content.

Effective use of contrast not only makes design more interesting but also more readable and navigable, facilitating information absorption.

Consistency

Consistency in graphic design is vital for building a recognizable and trustworthy brand. Consistency manifests in:

- *Color Palette*: Choosing a color palette that repeats across all digital platforms. This helps create a strong visual identity.

- *Typography:* Using a maximum of three fonts across all promotional materials. This maintains readability and design unity.

- *Style and Tone:* Keeping the same visual style and tone of voice. If the brand is playful, the design should reflect this through illustrations, animations, or casual layouts.

- *Design Elements:* Repeating graphics, icons, or motifs that become trademarks of the brand. This can include specific shapes, lines, or textures.

Consistency not only aids brand recognition but also builds trust and an emotional connection with the audience.

Visual Hierarchy

Visual hierarchy determines the order in which the user's eye perceives information. It's crucial for guiding the user through content intuitively. Here's how it can be implemented:

- *Size and Position:* Larger elements or those positioned at the top or center attract attention first. The headline should be the largest, followed by the subhead, then the body text.

- *Color and Contrast:* Use contrast to emphasize key points. A colored element on a monochromatic page will be immediately noticed.

- *Spacing:* Use of white (or negative) space to isolate and give importance to specific elements. This can also improve readability and visual breathing room.

- *Typography and Weight*: Varying the weight of text (bold, italic, underline) to create a hierarchy. For example, bold for a title, italic for a subhead, and normal for body text.

- *Images and Graphics:* Use images, icons, or graphics to break up text and guide the eye towards points of interest, especially if related to nearby text.
A good visual hierarchy not only enhances aesthetics but also communicative effectiveness, ensuring the main message is clear and conveyed quickly.

Practical Applications in Online Marketing

- *Websites and Blogs:* Apply contrast to highlight CTAs, use consistent typography to maintain brand identity across blog posts, and establish a visual hierarchy to guide visitors through the main information.

- *Social Media*: Images and videos should be designed with contrast to stand out in the feed, consistency for easy recognition, and visual hierarchy to communicate the message quickly.

- *Email Marketing:* Use contrast to make important sections stand out, maintain consistency in layout and branding for recognition, and set a hierarchy to ensure the recipient understands the email's purpose immediately.

- *Infographics and Presentations:* These tools must be visually engaging with effective use of contrast to separate information, consistency to keep interest, and clear hierarchy to facilitate data comprehension.

Conclusion

Graphic design in online marketing is much more than mere adornment; it's a powerful communication vehicle that, when used correctly, can transform how consumers perceive a brand. Through contrast, consistency, and visual hierarchy, a designer can create content that not only captures attention but also communicates effectively and builds a lasting bond with the audience. In the next chapter, we'll explore how these design basics can be further refined to create user experiences that not only inform but also inspire and deeply engage.

8.4: Creating Brand Identity:

How to Use Visual Marketing to Build and Strengthen Brand Identity

Building a brand identity that resonates with the audience requires a well-thought-out strategy, where visual marketing plays a crucial role. Brand identity isn't just a collection of logos and slogans; it's the visual and emotional essence that a company communicates to its audience. This chapter will explore how visual marketing can be used to build and strengthen this identity effectively.

Defining Brand Identity

Before starting with visual creation, it's essential to clearly define what the brand represents:

- *Values and Mission:* What are the brand's core values? What does it aim to do or change in the world?

- *Target Audience*: Who are the ideal consumers? What are their visual and cultural preferences?

- *Differentiation*: How does the brand distinguish itself from competitors in terms of vision, values, and product offering?

Visual Elements of Brand Identity

- *Logo:* Often the first point of contact with the brand. It should be simple, memorable, and represent the brand's values. A good logo should be versatile, scalable, and work well in black and white as well as in color.

- *Color Palette:* The chosen colors should evoke emotions and values the brand wants to convey. For example, green for sustainability, red for energy or passion.

- *Typography*: Font choice can communicate modernity, tradition, elegance, or casualness. It's important to choose fonts that are readable and consistent with the brand's image.

- *Graphic Elements:* This can include icons, symbols, or patterns that become recognizable and distinctive of the brand, like the shapes or icons Nike uses to reinforce the concept of movement and dynamism.

Visual Marketing Tools to Strengthen Brand Identity

- *Images and Photography:* Images are powerful storytelling tools. Using photographs that reflect the brand's values, whether they are product images, events, or people representing the target audience.

- *Illustrations and Graphics:* Illustrations can be used to make the brand more personal and unique. Illustration styles can range from minimalist and modern to detailed and narrative, reflecting the brand's personality.

- *Video and Motion Graphics*: Videos are excellent for telling stories and conveying complex messages engagingly. Stylistic consistency in terms of animations and transitions reinforces visual identity.

- *Social Media Design:* Each social platform should reflect the brand identity through layout, filters, and design of stories or posts. This includes the use of cover images, avatars, and the design of bios.

Practical Application of Visual Marketing

- *Cross-Platform Consistency:* All promotional materials, from emails to websites, from social media to product packaging, should reflect the same visual identity. This also includes materials like brochures, flyers, and billboards.

- *Visual Storytelling:* Using visual storytelling to create campaigns that not only sell products but also communicate values and missions. For example, a sustainability campaign might include images of pristine nature or eco-friendly production processes.

- *Feedback and Iteration*: Brand identity is not static. It must evolve over time. Gathering feedback and analyzing consumer behavior can guide updates and improvements to the visual identity.

Case Study: Strengthening Brand Identity

Let's take the example of an artisanal coffee brand that wants to reinforce its identity as sustainable and authentic:
- *Logo and Packaging:* A logo that incorporates natural elements like untreated coffee beans with a font that evokes authenticity and genuineness.

- *Social Campaign*: Using videos that show sustainable cultivation processes, interviews with local farmers, and images of products served in natural settings.

- *Events and Sponsorships*: Sponsoring ecological events with booths that reflect the brand's design, using recycled materials for displays and merchandise.

Conclusion

Visual marketing is a powerful tool for building and strengthening brand identity. Through the conscious and consistent use of visual elements, a brand can create an emotional connection with its audience, stand out in a crowded market, and build lasting loyalty. The key is to be authentic, consistent, and continuously evolving, listening to the audience and adapting to its expectations and cultural changes. In the next chapter, we'll explore how to integrate visual marketing with other marketing strategies to maximize impact and brand visibility.

8.5: Social Media Optimization:

Specific Techniques for Creating Platform-Optimized Visual Content

In the world of digital marketing, a presence on social media is crucial for reaching an audience and building a brand identity. However, each social platform has its own quirks and unspoken rules that affect the effectiveness of visual content. This chapter will explore specific techniques to optimize visual content for some of the most popular social platforms, ensuring the brand's message is not only seen but also remembered.

1. Instagram

Characteristics:
- *Visual-Centric:* Instagram is dominated by images and videos, with a strong focus on visual quality.
- *Feed and Stories*: Two main formats for posting, each with specific size recommendations.
Optimization:

- *Size and Format:* Ensure images and videos are in optimal resolution (1080x1080 for feed posts, 1080x1920 for stories). Use square or vertical formats.

- *Filters and Styles*: Utilize Instagram filters to maintain visual consistency. Creating a custom filter can strengthen brand identity.

- *Using Stories:* Add interactive elements like polls, questions, and countdowns to engage the audience.

- *IGTV and Reels*: Optimize for these formats with short, engaging, and often viral content. Use text and music to grab attention.

- *Hashtags and Geotags*: Use relevant hashtags and geotags to increase visibility.

2. Facebook

Characteristics:
- *Variety of Formats*: Posts, videos, stories, live streaming, and ad formats.
- *Community and Sharing*: Strong emphasis on user interaction and sharing.
Optimization:
- *Images and Videos*: Use high-quality images. Videos, in particular, have a higher engagement rate.

- *Format:* Images should be 1200x630 pixels, while videos shouldn't exceed 240 seconds for optimal visibility.
- *Overlaid Text*: Since videos are often viewed without sound, include overlaid text to convey key information.
- *Call to Action (CTA):* Include visible and inviting CTAs to boost interaction.
- *Events and Groups*: Optimize images for events and groups to attract participants and members.

3. Twitter (X)

Characteristics:
- *Brief and Concise:* Known for short tweets and a fast flow of information.
- *Multimedia*: Although text-based, using images, GIFs, and videos significantly boosts engagement.
Optimization:
- *Size:* Images should be 1200x675 pixels to appear large and eye-catching.
- *Visual Tweets*: Prefer tweets with images or videos for higher engagement.
- *GIFs and Memes*: Use GIFs or create memes that reflect humor or cultural moments to increase virality.

- *Visual Threads*: Create tweet threads that tell a story or concept with images or charts to maintain interest.

4. LinkedIn

Characteristics:
- *Professional and Business-Oriented*: Focused on professional networking and corporate branding.
- *Articles and Posts*: A mixture of short posts and in-depth articles.
Optimization:
- *Professional Images:* Use high-quality images that convey professionalism and expertise. Recommended dimensions are 1200x628 pixels.
- *Educational Videos:* Videos that convey knowledge or insights are highly valued.
- *Infographics*: Use infographics to present data or processes clearly and professionally.
- *Brand Consistency*: Maintain a strong visual identity reflecting the corporate brand.

5. Pinterest

Characteristics:

- *Visual Discovery:* Pinterest is a visual search platform where images are central.
- *Pins and Boards:* Users create and follow thematic "boards."

Optimization:

- *Size*: Images should be at least 600x900 pixels, with a 2:3 aspect ratio for vertical pins.
- *Detailed Descriptions:* Use detailed, keyword-rich descriptions to improve pin SEO.
- *Visual Styles:* Visual content should be inspirational and aspirational, with a strong emotional impact.
- *Thematic Boards*: Organize content into boards that reflect your target audience's interest categories.

Cross-Platform Strategies

- *Data Analysis:* Monitor the performance of visual content on each platform to understand what works best and adjust strategies accordingly.
- *Scheduling and Timing:* Post content when the audience is most active on each platform to maximize engagement.
- *Trends and Events*: Align visual content with seasonal trends, global events, or holidays to stay relevant.

Conclusion

Optimizing visual content for social media is not just about aesthetics but also strategy. Knowing the specifics of each platform and adapting content accordingly allows for effective audience reach and engagement, thus building a strong, recognizable brand identity. In the next chapter, we will explore how to integrate these visual strategies with content marketing tactics to create a cohesive and engaging narrative.

www.ingramcontent.com/pod-product-compliance
Lightning Source LLC
Chambersburg PA
CBHW071459220526
45472CB00003B/859